# Rhythmic Elegance

## A POETIC TREATISE ON OUR PLACE IN THE UNIVERSE

by

### ROBERT C SAUNDERS

Dynamically Activated, LLC

# What people are saying about
## *Rhythmic Elegance:*

"These poems are a reflection of the world's mindset. But the go beyond the issues that plague us today and make us question our humanity."

Jeanie Ferguson, housewife, mother

"This poet has a unique understand of the morass of man's struggles to deal with a fast-past ever changing world slipping deeper and deeper into self absorption and narcissism. This body of work is intellectually profound with an elegance of poetic turn."

Timothy Bodine, Owner, Operations Manager and Consultant of High-Impact Building Services

Book cover design by Bayprint

Photograph provided by Vanessa Protic of Demure-Lynn Photography

Publisher: Dynamically Activated, LLC
304 37th Ave N
Suite 310
St. Petersburg, Fl 33704
dynamicallyactivated@gmail.com

Visit the author website:
www.robertcsaunders.com
www.dynamicallyactivated.com

ISBN: 978-0-9982692-9-0

POETRY/GENERAL

Version: 2018.05.23

# Dedication

In memory of my parents Victor and Gloria Saunders, who did the best they could with what limited tools they had. The great spiritual legacy that we inherited was the virtue of a powerful work ethic. In reaching out for elegant things for their children, they raised our expectations both for ourselves and others. Thank you.

# OTHER BOOKS

# BY

# ROBERT C. SAUNDERS

Nurses Bred for Business:
*The Awakening Of Legions Of Nurse Entrepreneurs*

Dances in the Theater of the Mind

Foodie Dessertations:
*Bite Sized Recipes of Foodie-Licious Poetry*

# Table of Contents

# PREFACE

Of all the planetary bodies anywhere in our cosmos, why is it that the human race is so conflicted, so out of synch with majestic order on a colossal scale? By now, should we not have harmonized with the elliptical rhythm, the grand cadence and uniform elegance of a functional and ever expanding universe? This work is my contemplative journey through the human Dis-ease of our unlawfully restricted awareness and cosmic irresponsibility. Our realization of this state should illicit right actions, the transformative husbandry of our superpowers of willful individual and cumulative accountability and responsibility as sentient, spiritual beings. We must yet earn our citizenship as tenants in limitless space.

# Section 1

# Expanding Universal Awareness

## The stance

Before one can appreciate the divine nature of things, one must appreciate the basic natures, the etymology, syntax and nomenclature.

Before one can defend against the large and seemly insurmountable, one must identify and strategize against the small so as to gain their mastery quantified and recountable.

Before intimate familiarity with the gigantic, must hunt down the meek and mighty processes elemental to the microscopic.

Before knowing divine, know self divinely.

Before college there was kindergarten, all knowledge building on itself pliable and never hardened.

Go back to the formative basics then, so as to ascertain the greatness and smallness of men.

# The Recalcitrant

What could be worse in cerebral chatters, than to be stubborn about empty headed matters?

To staunchly assume a position that yields no treasure, vigorously defend a mindset that defies good measure.

To dig ones heels into entrenched position, that results in loss of life for its lamentable volition.

To ignore the nature of fantabulous heavenly realities so far beyond us, is to deny all else in the face of mounting evidence that should redeem thus.

This is the sad, pathetic fate of the recalcitrant as even mules have good reasons for their stubbornness.

## My Skies hued

Skylike ponderings colored by bold, brilliant splashing,
blues of self limiting doubts, grays of troubling
ignorance, violets of short-sighted, self knowledge
among the dashings, against stratospheric ideals are the
splintered, blackened, charred crashings.

Reddish yellow rays of hope burn through cerebral
atmospheric cloud bursts, once again drenching the
parched soil of possibility bestirring anew what human
growth thirsts.

Ahh! So greenly hued inside, good fruitage is yielded
outside.

# How blessings work thru

They reign down from strong cosmic sources,
emanating en mass, powerfully, dutifully beseeched in
prayerful beam emitting forces.

Tumbling upon the heights, all earth's children
deserving, from the Father of the Celestial Lights,
devoted and unswerving.

To conceptualize only one country cornering blessings
so esoterica, restrictive statements accorded like "God
bless North America!"

This planet is already too tiny to contain all that is
divinely rich and good in tow, only our bad actions and
poor decisions will block its flow.

# I Sorry

So much as I have caused you pain, obviously I didn't
mean to make tears flow again.

Really like to see you smile as friends,
reason would have us make amends.

You know that what is yours is mine and mine is yours,
a symbol of the trust this underscores.

So melt away the pain and dispel old fears,
I will make greater effort not to be the source
of future tears.

I Sorry is my sincere and real apology.

# Transparency

Goodness does not hide behind closed doors
and demand its rights aired apparent,
it deals in just acts of kindness inherent,
speaks by the beauty that practices
self control transparent.

Lives in invisible vessels and principles,
worries not about surveillance of police, CIA,
or FBI to spy out criminality or brutality for surety,
as its nature is to make each a responsible enforcer
of homeland security.

Transparency knows humility's footsteps
rejecting violence and drug possession,
clean rap sheets of moral character
as a natural progression.

It cleans its own planetary messes,
avoids the amoral clutter of sexual excesses.

It's actions so fair, so just, so nice, so peaceful,
so plain to see, drilling down to full transparency.

# The Power of She

Without she, no we, couldn't tell from the
direction of society's vision blurred,
lack of long range clarity feeds impropriety.

It is in the best interest of humanity to value
her childbearing wonder, while civilizations have
faded for lack of recognizing this blunder.

Wars and violence destroy good men who
cherish the uniqueness of she, strong shoulders
and testosterone flexing necessitate healthy females,
help her be all that she can be.

When she wins, we all win, any other way is abject sin,
misogyny, chauvinism, detract and demean,
sex trafficking demoralizes multiplied
to the obscene.

Justice and fairness maintain the import of womanly awareness, pornography obliterates sexual objectivity, entertainment centered rape and abuse, teaches selfish unreality, deifies unfaithfulness, makes devotion a cheapened formality.

Warped and twisted notions, alters she views, boys feeding on more horrors of brutalized women making the news.

She now demonized, reduced, rejected, what is the answer? History often ignored is so often resurrected.

All the while ignored are the galaxies of relationship ecstasies that she confers, dissecting the loss of her humaneness bestirs.

Our Work is cut out for us facing in pedigree, the loss of she is loss of civilized we.

## Flunked Pre-Kindergarten

How many university educated still have not learned
the lessons of their pre-K yester years?

Don't take what is not yours without asking,
don't touch, push or shove others or be held
accountable for last thing.

Your privates are yours in front and in back,
this envelope should never be pushed just because
others self-control lack.

Don't be a tyrant by violent collusion,
no weapons, no bullying, no taking amidst
this concocted confusion.

No lying conniving, or stone cold extortion,
no conveniently sidestepping consequences
in surreptitious abortion, humbly saying sorry when
you're wrong or add to worldwide distortion.

To expand the intellect must equally expand moral
character quotient, truthfulness, solidarity, kindness,
justice, all things that make good citizens quite potent.

Schools should exist soon for such belated remediation,
not too late to start learning these missed lessons
despite one's current station.

Righting wrongs of the past is what we should all be
about, for those still causing trouble, no milk
and cookies, send straight to time out.

# Throw Myself Away

I left myself in the junk stack, got off track,
procrastinations suicide, non productive formaldehyde.

The stuff of life drew my attention away from real
emotions, aspirations by extension to useless devotions.

Start only looking forward and forgetting to look back,
the richness of my past has since turned moldy and
black. an otherwise great life now stinks because I
trashed it.

Now, to pick through piece by piece to salvage and
unify, the longings, unattended, reconnect and verify.

Big journey ahead, I cannot deny,
won't give up and die inside, got to try.

Learn from this, don't pick and choose amongst
all that drives you, unify your vision, your hobby,
your work, your play, your music, your worldview.

Don't get this right and life ends you, pained
with lack of fulfillment, knives driven through.

## Minds Dating

Two curious minds prospect and inspect,
female deflect male circumspect.

Meld their intellectual hues, synaptic
convergence of divergent views.

Dendritic connections expand as two choose
future direction as one experiential entity,
emotional make ups and adaptive intensity.

Neuronal baggage outweighed by a
spiritual happiness coefficient,
a high workability index makes
uniting, multiplying quite elegant.

Nothing casual about this anthropologically
intrinsic phenomenon, procreational
analysis and legacy postulations.

This is serious human specie highly ordered relating, propagation business in the form of minds dating.

## Victorious

Be careful of the goals and plans you are pursuing,
with no direction could be your undoing.

Draft a strategy on tap, keep it brewing,
drink up more rounds of knowledge,
don't stop what your pursuing.

When you invest the time as all champions are doing,
eat, sleep and breath the purpose that you're renewing.

Past and present failures now are the fertilizer
of future success most glorious, so you must
stay on the course of all who are victorious.

## Shaded by Trust

Trust, it does live in the moment,
considerate of past promises
and commitment.

Future burns bright as implicit confidence
in all that is expected to come, additive
standing to principles multiplied
to its sum.

When foolishness has been tested,
deeps thoughts inspected, properly
corrects despite rationality
being deflected.

Knows a good thing when it sees it,
wise enough, decisive enough
to seize it.

Cultivated in restorative peace,
fosters a body of trustees in the least.

Water regularly to full maturity, until
large branches of free expression grow,
bears more assurance and conviction
than one could possibly know.

Thusly moved to seek contentment and tranquility
under its mature refreshing shade, so powerfully
fostered in its trustworthy virility.

So unifying, so strong, so positive, so rare,
so beautiful, so loving a quality as
trust all can share.

Grow as much of this rare breed as
possible in the acres of life.

## Cold Blooded Numbers

Cold realities drip straight from numbered
buttons symmetrically faced, in this joint
truth in mathematical flow
has been cased.

Prejudices as the source of world derision scatters,
singling out the practicality in all matters.

Marching through formulaic brew divisible,
the basis of all stances, multiplicable
in mathematical parlances.

Clarity and light flushed out in random
number generators, scientifically notated,
logarithmically charted, now an array
to infinity rotated.

A function keyed, mowing down whole statistical
demographics aggressive with calculator passion,
the digital sight of fingered menaces pull
the trigger on causational ration.

Excited purely by the computationalistic,
seperating the astrophysically expansive
from the mystic.

# Random Not So Much

Random is not so random as can be affected
by our decision tree, by relationship grids
and what self-control algorithms decree.

Example, "officer, he hit me out of the blue without
provocation!" So conveniently left out the racial slurs
thus made, one in string of many angry mindless rants,
intentionally so, now "a not so random" price is paid.

# I'm a get prolific

So, the machinery amped up this odyssey,
now run through the greenery, maximize
that productivity.

Do more to strategy, lay tracks, align facts,
progress road stretch movement made in
modesty, coal is burning, smoking,
pressurize creativity.

One idea, two ideas, and the wheels of thought
processes congeals cycling ideas, now 10,
specifics of purposeful intentions
leading us past inertial passivity,
the how turned into when.

I think I can, I think I'll plan to do this all again.
The general to the specific, from mundane
to ah-ha, watch out coming through,
I'm a get prolific.

# Please Judge Me

Don the robes oversized and black,
white haired wig and gavel to whack.

Weigh the evidence of my
actions that constitutes me.
Have I exceeded my boundaries?
Proved a true menace to society?
Should I be incarcerated for my improprieties?
Or paraded in the streets for immorality?

Legal precedence beckoning conscience,
how we elevate ethically our sisters and brothers,
each month, each day, each hour, each second.

Better to answer the plaintive cry that justice fights,
than side with guilty defendants who insist on rights.

Have I proved to be a good citizen of land, sky and sea?
That I could preserve it in eternal uphold
royal natural decree.

If my thinking is perverse, bad practices stout,
not much to deliberate if my guilt is fact
without a doubt.

I won't hide behind legal banter,
to jurisprudence I'll give deference.

Spare me the sentimentality if I perpetrated wicked
deeds. I want the full brunt of law and principle
weighed out blindly, whether there is community
service or electric chains is where you'll find me.

Don't strip me indecently of personal accountability,
I only ask in all fairness and impartiality,
please judge me.

## Predatory Strut

All the wolves on parade, rapaciously advances,
circumstances jugular, wildlife dances.

Something amiss, sense of danger foreboding,
behind smiles of insecurity hide
death in sheep's clothing.

The sneer, the growl effecting,
fomenting a sense of loathing.

Don't for a moment discount their danger pulsed,
taste of your blood is in the air,
primal hunger results.

Have enough sense to evade their rampages
or be the lament of future sages.

## Can't Get this Thing Kick Started

I can't do it, keep pulling at that string,
energy to kick start, internal desire, brrrr!
so cold, so much grassy thoughts
initiatives to mow down.

I need to clip through and ponder greener pastures in
view, current armies of tall bladed emotionally
charged impasses eskewed.

Mindset resistant to change, fertilized with fears,
growing unreasonable doubts daily,
keep tugging, new plugging.

Cerebral carburetor fuel perhaps mixed too
rich with idealism, insufficient air of pragmatism,
chocking off the sparkplugs of ideas, poorly
idling, sputtering on the frequented
sidewalk of unrelenting reservations,

maybe today is not the day to move stalled engines
of imaginations, only wishing to drive blades awhirl
with sharpened possibility, propelling progress.

# Gun-Like Ones Among Us

Gun control issues are only a symptom of violent
human outcroppings that drive increasing inability
to solve domestic disputes.

Peaceably? is the big ball that we're dropping,
hair trigger firing, short patience fuses
with much faulty mental wiring.

Volatile anger fills the void of a world of useless
peace treaties while stockpiling magazine clips,
the rata tat tat of endless offenses is that to which
we must ultimately come to grips.

Forgive and forget can't still be
"I'll bide my time and get you yet."

If your house is declared a non-violent zone
then no one within it can or should
remain anger prone.

No such thing as men of war and simultaneously men
of peace?! Any other way is equivocal to say the least.

Assault rifle minds eventually translate
to external gunplay, may be tomorrow,
could be today.

Guns kill people because gun-like minds are
the birthing chambers by extension of this
natural progression, a deadly tool married
to an innocent tool user? Try selling that
to the victim's family at the
funeral procession.

This not complicated, just manifest cold technological
human defiance, mixed with billion dollar companies
amassing firearms reliance.

How convenient to direct automation at
the 9mm of our prejudicial darkness,
our grenade launcher jealousies,

our machine gun racisms, our
semiautomatic irrational fears

Bump stock desires stoke weaponized demands,
now how do you take guns from itchy,
violence prone hands?

Many will dismiss these truisms as nonsensical fuss,
and will fiercely stockpile home and hearth as
gun-like ones among us.

## Idea Incubator

Fat ones, skinny ones, really really long ones,
finished and unfinished, no less important,
no more diminished.

These ideas birthed in a curious mind,
problems seeking solutions close encounters
hatched of the bird kind.

Why do ideas hatch? Where do they originate?
The fact is that the mind does what it does.
It loves to propagate, germinate, co-create,
this is its state.

50, 100, 1,000 impactful successes addresses its
universal cranial essence spinning infinities,
don't block creative flow, boundless in propensities.

# Keep Track

Set the sail on your boat right, check the sailor's log,
for your journeys to maintain insight, recheck,
align with actions, keep ones focus right.

Where you are where is it where you want to be?
Living life as you were meant to run free?
Have you gone as far as discerning eyes can see?

Be most careful or one can get off track,
don't look behind, look forward,
check for momentum's breeze,
not possible to do all that you please.

Take into account waves of adversity,
undercurrents of doubts and fears,
driving turbulent dis-ease and
windswept bravado.

Time is less mindful, regularly track your position on matters against the constellation of all things whole, while exercising faith in what is beyond our capacity to control.

Keep life's direction relevant and clearly focused within, so that you will be deserving of accrued success when your ship comes in.

# Never Lose It

Undeniable faith pacing,
lines in the fabric of life tracing,
what was once held in the heart
conscientious ponderings effacing.

No longer engendering genuine strength
tearing what is real from non-real apart,
toppling to an end emotional derelicts
before fairness had its start.

Before one loses their soul in this
spiritually windswept corrosive swathe,
determine to be rocklike, indefatigable
in never, never, never losing faith.

## Bleeding Eyes

Blood viscous, our existence represented,
in pierced eyes pained by the graphic pictures
life paints unrelented.

Battered wives bleeding by words, by fists,
by emotional oppression, child prostitution
and boy soldiers an outcropping of exploitive
social economic depression.

How much crushing poverty can one take?
How much war and bloodshed can
human eyes endure in its wake?

Tortured eyes suffering daily dark tragedies chilled
when mother's eyes scream at stillborn children,
no closer to answering the what? the why? the when?

Stop please, no more sorrow, no more death,
justice cries inside, a world of humans denied
about to go blind, at the terror that has been
perpetrated against all our bleeding eyes.

# Well Rooted

How well our ways are deeply rooted in our history,
culture, traditions well suited?

The sum of what we are now is the totality of
our future, make present our rich past,
before we were trees, thick and strong,
bearing fruits of labor at last.

We were seeds planted in the soil of generations,
watered by vision, taking root in burgeoning
wealth of nations.

The deeper down we reached into what we came from,
the higher and taller we grew our parts, our branches,
our bark, our leaves, all greater than the sum.

Keep reaching down into ancestral innateness and
keep reaching forward to the stars that greatness suited,
where others will conclude that your success is
a result of being well-rooted.

## Plague

Images change and thoughts seeking an outlet,
lacking expression, imagination at the brink of
depression.

How does one release that which already
has no boundaries in the creative realm?
Yet cannot manifest itself in
the physical realm?

I seek relief from fantastic frights of fantasy possession,
rambunctious and fighting, dynamic delusions of
creative grandeur, experiencing nightly progression.

Ambitions bumps are spreading inside the soul,
pandemic radical paradigms shifting,
success-mindedness heir apparent
in artistically licensed gifting.

# Extraneous Thoughts

On top of the head are radical thoughts as hair
blowing in the wind, heads juxtaposed,
fleeting thoughts rescind, gray-haired
thoughts driven by hard informalities within.
This is a zoo!

Wild erratic contemplations running amok,
"no self-control for me" they scream in wild abandon.

Reality relents like a star on a shopping spree,
a tree gone off the trunk, our uncontrolled desires
parading aimlessly.

Oh well, they are, after all unconnected thoughts.

# No Evolutionary Quirk

Most definitely made every given sum played,
a matter more of creator haterade.

Just as the universe orchestrated became the ancient
timepiece of God, so man and woman designed of
engineered biological machine parts, same mind,
same hearts, same orchestrated nod.

Human kind still cooling from the cast thus molded,
time will soon reveal built in accountability due
due design purposes unfolded, life's DNA
written in genetic parlance exploded.

He plus she squared to the roots of providential apogee,
qualified in quantitative and rotational degree,
the more galactic facts analyzed the more
criminal the evolutionary absurdity.

# Growing Up into Prejudices

Morphing into misery, the warped function of our
environmental conjunction, the edge of the strife, the
tip of hard years, courage beaten out of us, now we
embody the sum of our fears, some wanted to be
cowboys or astronauts, no limits, no tears.

What we wanted when young is not necessarily now
who we are growing up into our deep seated prejudices.

Have strengthened by far the media showcases,
flexed prejudicial muscles, vocalize racist chants,
as hated classes and police tussles.

What we are groomed for in silence,
is soon all that grownups will loudly speak,
more loudly than the anemic peace and unity
that we sheepishly say we seek.

## Last Rights

A memorial is being held for the last rights of our
humanity, the right to have an opinion on ageless
morality, the right to stand for something
meaningful and die by its finality.

The right to fairness in an ordained, Godly way,
the right to non-violence in our life's work and play.

Right to be inflexible on universal principles true,
right to not have to choke down any intolerable,
corrupted, idealogical brew.

If there are more of these rights, they are lost and long
dead, it's end located with the rest of
the ill fated that bled.

## Too Far

Too far north is south, too far east is west.
How much ethical distance traveled is best?
How far is too far before a line is drawn?
Can we just give it a rest? Pursuing
rights too far what's left?

What seems to good is often bad, tolerance
taken too far makes many mad, intolerance
taken to far makes me sad, life with some
moral boundaries makes me glad.

Someone must reason for the unreasoning.
Be a selfless force among the selfish. Be a humbling
force among the arrogant. Say enough is enough,
drawing a line in the sand for the belligerent.

Stand on sure footing so as to rise above the indifferent
and those who selfishly take without permission,
ignore the internal lawyer pleading for conscience.

Muster courage in a societal machinery of fear.
Open minds to perfect ideals heaven sent,
as well as close minds to those whose bad
intentions are dangerously hell bent.

Be uncommonly good for those who ignore
grim reality and uncommon sense lack.

Just ahead on the too far train is a sign that reads,

Precipice ahead, too late to turn back!!!

# Recipes for Disaster

For a deadly summer medley what bad decisions would
you concoct?

It seems human nature to want, not need to pandora's
cupboard unlock.

Too many forbidden fruits create many a nasty mix
of assorted jams greed and bitter jealousies, add
just a smig of inner turmoil and a dash of
dopey to enhance the insecurities.

Fully ripened phobias simmering in a vat of its own
juices, has made a lot of great plans the seasoning of
many cooked gooses.

Mix fanaticism with 2 handfuls of humanities darkest
fears, and under heat low tolerance can quickly come
to a boil in genocide, blood and tears.

Substitute equal portions of reality for fantasy,
lack of discipline and unrestrained will, then
serve cold to young minds in sociopathic
portions with bad habits, making
terrible decisions yet still.

This is just a sampling of what people do just
because they feel that they should, not even
devil worshippers could make
recipes this good.

# The undone

Not the undead,
just lay that to bed.

No, the undone zealously starts but leaves
all projects half done, in love with the idea of
beginning to explore, attention dementia checks
follow thru at the door.

There is dignity in staying focused till the finish,
Otherwise, the value of time continues to
diminish.

At death, what will the undone's epitaph read?
"He had the capacity for greatness, too bad he
could never muster the staying power to
fully succeed."

There is might in the finish and victory in the hard fight won, glory is in the completion, only shame and dishonor in the undone.

# Window stills

Look out the window at all the walking mosaics
of "your so wrong and only I have rights," nobody
wants to be lied to yet so many oblivious to keen
insights.

Promenading life decision courses as windowed
stills, each a snapshot in time that bespeak
contrasting extremes of broken wills, each
a philosophical and religious earthly body
that mills, A deafening roar of stillness that
by gravitational consensus shrills.

# Cosmic thoughts

Wait! How can we be the masters of our fate if
we haven't mastered ourselves?

Have yet to see anyone running around
complaining about being plagued by
massive self discipline.

Some may think were such hot stuff as a planet,
I side with others who also see a big hot mess.

I am waiting for this panicked cry:
Help police!! My neighbors are grossly unselfish!
Hurry before they commit some selfless act of
conscience. Or worse, they may exercise their
right to not impose their will on me!! (So scary!)

Why is everything backwards if were the planets
forward thinkers?

Why is there a space program when we in so much
trouble in what little space we do occupy
and influence?

Let us take a commercial break from being
currently spaced out and instead dance to
planetary spinning, stretch our cosmic
awareness of just how out of step we
are with founding principles of higher
astrophysical bidding.

Before we whimsically do what we want,
let us find our ethical cadence and do
what we ought, elevate our actions,
our minds in time with cosmic thought.

# Burn the war garments

No to war boots
No to war shoes
No to weapons of war
No to platforms of weaponization leading to
radicalization.
No to war helmets
No to sexy war fatigues, haven't we been fatigued
enough by all the blood spilled?
No to war paint
No more war books, they are not serving us other than
grim reminders of
of how insanely stupid war is and the forces that
nurture and foment it.
No more war treaties! (What "peace" treaties really are)
No more war games, just perfect dress rehearsals for the
Act 1, Scene 1of
the real thing.

Yes to peace researchers, peace manufactures, and peace mongers
with their peace profiteering again.
Yes to peace boot camps teaching advanced peace techniques
Yes to peace wardrobes just in case we have a mass break out of peace, "madam, you look just heavenly in that peace dress!"
Yes to monetized peace initiatives

# Where loyalty is from

In a world failing due to the lack of loyalty,
where so far of track that this really broils me.

Search and see do so most thoroughly, Is it
in you? Is it not in me? Is it a hereditary
unexpressed genus quality?

Where ever it is, whenever it may be found,
humanity must identify and amass it if it
plans to stick around.

No coincidence that tranquility and
universal harmony rhymes with
loyalty.

Where either in synch with loyalty or in synch with
death, "it is our choice" will be said by the
disloyal with their dying breath.

The issue is not if God will do right by us,
No, will we do right by....?

It can't be bought but it can be taught
if we ask nicely of the authority from
whom it emanates from.

A word with the powerful

People who live in glass houses are
told not to throw stones, should
also realize the power of words
to heal or break bones.

Never be hypnotized by personal greatness,
should only feel the demoralizing weight
of delayed justices lateness.

What matters more than position and pomp,
Is listening and responding to the roar of
wickedness next reckless stomp.

What is that rancid stench? It is the ignorance
and inaction of the powerful.

# Cosmic cadence

Astrophysical objects waltzing in elegant advances,
circular form and grace in rotational step with
celestial dances.

Night sky jewels stealing away,
magnificent in rhythmic synchrony,
the mass of each ones morality
perceived in orderliness of
gravitational harmony.

Imperceptible steps seemingly motionless
a commissioned jeweled menagerie. What
if each one of us would join in the
movement of stellar peace?
Radiating nebulous joy?
Sharing a sufficient all
encompassing societal
binding?

60 / Robert C. Saunders

Enriching others in a billion lifetimes of
thermonuclear release?

Then a true fusion of humanity with
luminous universal valence, a never
ending system of stable orbits
in cosmic cadence.

# When love is late

Just 5 seconds past another school shooting

Just 4 seconds past race riots and hateful brutality.

3 seconds past multi-victim car bombing with no
rhyme or reason.

2 seconds before and another child abduction
as if we are stuck in sex trafficking season.

1 second before 4 planes were used as weapons
of mass destruction.

Love just received a letter from badness:
"See what happens when I am on time and your
Just seconds too late"

# Everything is Religion

Vegan-ism
Intellectual-ism
Spirit-ism
Sex-ism
Human-ism
Politic-ism
Scholastic-ism
Favorite-ism
Cynic-ism
Race-ism
Material-ism
Monetary-ism
Food-ism
Cash is king-ism
Body-ism
Muscle-ism
Animal-ism
Weapon-ism

Self-ism

War-ism

Car-ism

House-ism

Violent-ism

Terror-ism

Love-ism

Recidiv-ism

Ostrac-ism

## STD origins

How many STD's don't start out 1$^{st}$ with mental dis
eases and moral itemized deficiencies?
The syphilis of unfaithfulness
The gonorrhea of poor mental faculty
The H.I.V. of weakened resolve
The full blown A.I.D.S. of unrestrained
passions passed on freely

Fortunately, there are some powerful Sulfa drugs that
can slow its progression:
Sulfa control
Sulfa restraint
Sulfa sacrifice
Sulfa determination
Sulfa responsibility
Sulfa accountability

(*Presently there is an international shortage of social ethics, propriety and basic human decency, those infected may have to formulate own measured dosing.)

Why accelerating beyond pandemic proportions? Pornographic illnesses spread by the virulent bed bug "Me first" and the explosive head lice identified as "My rights."

Regardless, some feel STD's are so worth it still, for added measure, all that bonus misery and mounting death for but a few moments of illicit pleasure.

Social picture

I'm here to paint a certified picture,
of you helping me and me helping you
get richer.

In ways beyond money and time,
elevates to a place above the daily grind.

It is about supporting the cause and purpose
that lifts us, since were made in the image of
one that gifts us.

Put down antagonism's gun, now is the time
to act and think and move as one.

With one thought, one man, in step, with one plan
regal and dignified as principles kept.

What is our true inner constellation like?
Contemplate these deeply as we move through
starry nights and days on this planetary
rocket bike.

We must do this for all as we face
down our own extinction,
expand the vocabulary of our moral diction.

Singularly rip open the mind and heart for
a total multi-organ transplant, trade up
from arrogance to humility unworkable
ways supplant.

Radicalizing the place were our desire meets scripture,
it is only here that we will enjoy a sustainably
changed and rearranged social picture.

# Section 2

## Responsible Cosmic Citizenship

# Relativistic Everything

As inhabitants of the universe we graduate to the title celestial beings that exist on a celestial planet moving in an orderly fashion in relation to other celestial entities. All of this is in obeisance to celestial mechanical principles that govern the material universe. These principle or constants coordinate billions of heavenly galaxies into a cohesive precision time piece. I have come to observe similar success principles that govern the very measure of what success in the human realm entails in terms of health, wealth and happiness. Failures also seem to work in galactic clusters having strong biochemical affinities.

In **physics, relativistic** mechanics refers to mechanics compatible with special relativity (SR) and general relativity (GR). It provides a non-quantum mechanical description of a system of particles, or of a fluid, in cases where the velocities of moving objects are comparable to the speed of light.

Einstein sought to find a unified mathematical explanation of everything at the macroscopic and the microscopic level. I have taken poetic license in using words to accomplish the same thing and whether we choose to acknowledge it or not, we as humans live at the microscopic level relative to exponentially magnificent macroscopic realities.

Social relativistic physics compatibly equates to the velocity of human activities and positive or negative effects of each individuals celestial mass exerted.

Relativistic ethics, in this context, highlights the quantum mechanical effects of the exercise personal celestial conduction on all that is matter. If our celestial equation of what constitute right conduct is not thought thru, it can induce negative electromagnetic effects and nuclear forces out of harmony with universal constants.

Relativistic morality, in this context, amplifies the massive gravitational impact that each individuals principle of judging right and wrong can exert upon other bodies in positive or negative, micro and macroscopic proportions.

Relativistic social consciousness, in this context, expounds on powerful biochemical covalent bonding involving the mutual sharing we have with all other celestial beings occupying planet earth and the stable balance of attractive and repulsive forces that will either unite us into one fully responsible and fully accountable specie or catastrophically end us for lack of clear shared vision.

Relativistic Inequalities showcases that throughout the universe inequalities are inherent to all celestial elements, systems and processes. It is a mathematical and astrophysical peace accord that promotes harmony instead of discord. The human body is also designed around advantageous inequalities as a homeostatic peace treaty. Each system, each body part, each cell accepts the other as different, unique, competent and essential to the purposeful, smooth functioning of a unified organism. Animals, from insects to elephants relish inequality and have, in effect, signed a universal non compete clause with each other that they will contractually work for the good of the planet and symbiotically unify on differences and balance each ones weaknesses with the other's strengths. Yet, humans, by numerous societal metrics, cannot seem to grasp these same higher advantageous permutations of inequality and remain grounded in negatively charged emotions of pride, envy, pity and disgust toward each other. There culturally differentiated prejudices, ambivalent attitudes and distinct cerebral activations are the basis for miscalculated efforts at making everyone and everything in their universe equal. As provocative as it sounds, it lacks correlation with universal constitutional precepts and is demonstratively and dehumanizingly unworkable.

A relativity of everything is what I grasp from Einstein's theory. Mass, energy and speed of all celestial bodies are mathematically interrelated and have a valid and correct formulaic expression. Planets and stars move relative to each other in the symphony of universal constants of gravitation, electromagnetism, strong and weak nuclear forces. The human body's operational processes are inextricably linked to said constants and can only perform relative to such. The mass, energy and speed of the sphere of human thoughts, mental powers and decision making processes are also definitively shaped by inertial celestial forces. Societal laws seek a celestial nomenclature in formulaic address of the mass effects of our actions toward each other. Tempers the speed of justice and gauges the exertion of energy on our moral agency and the payment of social currency toward each other in valid and correct expression.

Problems arise when we as celestial beings diverge from the spiritual nature of working celestial principles as constants. Our planet and our eternal destiny as a specie is inextricably linked to the celestial presence of the sun and neighboring star clusters for all its life-sustaining properties. Their mass, speed and energy are tailored to govern our planets movement with relatively kind gravitational consistency, electromagnetic devotion and peaceful thermonuclear accord. A master principle emerges that glues the universe together is that of violation of one principle is violation of all principles. This master principle bears all the contextual facets of love. Our lives are positively shaped by its daily conveyance of joy, happiness contentment and measure of celestial peace. These bodies are impartial and fair in that they consistently apply sound judgement to their movements, considering the magnitude of all that they are relative to. Most living things on planet earth are in turn locked into the chronobiological cycle of light and darkness which powerfully impact our physical, mental and behavioral processes. When we decidedly attempt to fight these sleep/wake cycles, every cell of our being makes known its intolerance to such unwise determinations by manifest dis eases and conditions. Some of these penalties include sleep disorders, obesity, diabetes, depression, bipolar disorders, etc. Human societal dis eases and debilitating world conditions relate to self inflicted ignorance of celestial laws governing thought and behavioral movements of our most basic biological and moral constitution. Individually incongruent failings in the arena of expressed principled kindness, devotion, peace translates to global failures of escalating radicalization, warfare, sex trafficking, etc relative to mass societal hypocrisies or pretenses.

## Societal Hypocrisies and Manifest Destiny

Hypocrisy: 1. A feigning to be what one is not or to believe what one does not. 2. Behavior that contradicts what one claims to believe or feel. 3. The false assumption of an appearance of virtue or religion.

As vast and complex as the universe is, it is completely transparent in the principality of its exerted movements and never deviates from clear and purposeful intention. The celestial bodies we occupy also mesh with universal transparency, holding to one established truth in all its anabolic and catabolic processes balanced to maintain life. It is only on planet earth that a word had to be coined express this celestial societal paradox and there are many.

What earthly society says in principle is divorced from what earthly society actually does even with sanctioning of laws and penalties:

It says it has laws against murder yet murder is elevated, industrialized, and escalating on a global scale thru the things reflecting malignancies in our psyche and abhorrently weaponize what we pleasurably fixate upon in the theater of the mind.

It says it has deep faith and convictions in sanctity of grander divine precepts yet religious practitioners fight the bloodiest wars and do things that make atheists puke. These use a celestial awareness of need for right thought and purpose driven action as a scapegoat to excuse universally grotesque cancerous habits and attitudes and justify schizophrenic violence against perceived opposers.

It says it loves the transparency of truth and hates being lied to yet it binges on debilitating lies and purges self evident realities. Gives pageantry to dishonest propaganda, gluttonously imbibes immoral untruth and parties with reckless endangerment. Thus, ignoring the gravitational Newtonian physics of each untruthful action having an unalterable equal and opposite reaction.

It says it wants equitable world governance yet rejects any idea of an inertial influence of a final authority of any kind that reflects prideful arrogance over being told what to do and how to live. This incongruent notion defies the resonance a workable, functional society ever submitting to the relativity of a universalized final authority. When the human body's cellular structures endure discord long enough and no longer respond to dictates of DNA's authority, cell death ensues. Then when enough cells can no longer replicate and die off, the untimely demise of the organism is undeniable as the stages of death are initiated. The only freedom that cellular components have in the long run is to freely adhere to genetic principle. Effective leadership as a force for good is only relevant to a celestial society when intrinsically balanced with effective good citizenship in a shared accountable and predictable rotation.

## Manifest Destiny

In the context of this treatise, manifest destiny is transparency bearing fruitage, formative and summative actions of inner truths that exerts its relative influence external physical matter. Although a direct study of the interior of the sun is impossible, insights into the conditions; temperature, composition and motions of gas within the sun, may be gained by observing oscillating waves, rhythmic inward and outward motions of its visible surface. Similarly, the seismic waves generated by earthquakes can be studied so as to ascertain the inner workings of the earth's interior. The human body has complex internal and psychoactive structures whose functional states and dis eases even now may only be deduced from observing external developments such as fever, nausea, vomiting, pain, swelling, etc. Societal dis eases all start with the basic unit of society the individual. Each autonomous celestial entity moving about the planet is too complex so as to speak authoritatively to predictive patterns of thought and ideation. We can however draw direct conclusions empirically from by individually and collectively observed oscillating behaviors and rhythmic outward behavioral motions as clues of predictive patterns. The following are noted global consistencies:

- Internal is external and external is internal; bad habits shape behavioral and criminal policy instead of policy putting away bad behavior and criminals.

- Disfiguring private practices ultimately manifest publicly as horrid shame that no one should be proud of.

- Abuse of personal freedoms behind closed doors graduates to freedoms of others abused in open forum.

- Super heated criminal minds violently explode into criminally riddled rap sheets of escalating propensity and full expression.

- Radicalized internal perversions seek radical outlets for their inevitable physical expression.

- Extremist problem potentials equate to extremisms pro terrorist solutions

- Those bereft of their own humanity see no problem stealing the identity of others.

- Self exploitations nuclear weaknesses become a thermonuclear trigger of globally addictive exploitation of others.

- The bracketed internal miscalculations of immoral and unethical justifications become the root causes of inhumane behaviors to the meanest.

- Inner microcosmic anarchist realities warps into masked specter of escalating macroscopic, multifaceted world terrorism.

Central to all such manifest destinies is the selfish and irresponsible unawareness of the ensuing repercussions of internal disarray. In the long run, this is pure ignorance of the master principle of love. Violation of one celestial principle is ultimately a violation of all principles. Remove just one gear from a time piece and it's function is adversely affected, even causing it not to function at all. The medical community is not as eager as they once were to simply cut out body parts that appeared to be the problem. Why? Because medical science still cannot create a suitable replacement for original body parts. Cutting off body parts often creates more problems than it solves. The free radical damage of violating one celestial principle is as exponentially devastating to societal health. One act of self violation sets off a systemic chain reaction of violations that will adversely affect other human bodies. Humans violating the rights of others humans and animals leads us to humans and animals now negatively producing planetary violations. Violating the planets delicate and poorly understood systems for the support of all life will quickly end us up in celestial insolvency and irrelevancy.

Human society has fashioned itself as the masters of their own fate. We may be at the wheel of our destiny, however, we drive without license or insurance. Our perceptions are impaired and our competencies as yet are underdeveloped to say the least. Who told us that we have ultimate control of industrial grade planetary destiny machinery? Why have we mass produced such delusions of grandeur? How is it we believe ourselves so smart? What universal metric are we utilizing to make that determination as under aged drivers barely out of diapers and yet to be properly schooled?

# Definition Shortcomings

As a relatively young celestial specie we are still barely out of temporal infancy in comparison to the estimated age of the known physical universe. In effect, we are still just toddlers learning to walk in paths of universal submission to fantastic quantum mechanical manifestations that should leave us in awe. Despite being at an age of great cognitive, emotional and social development we are still unsteady and immature in our cadence and posture. We are far too confident in our assertions of who we are and pompous in our perceived entitlement to operational phenomenon that is beyond our developmental grasp at this time. Our universal prekindergarten lessons in humility will begin shortly as we must be put in touch with our great insignificance relative to the dynamic machinery of a vast celestial timepiece. One lesson will be that our human identity is only valid relative to our individual and societal celestial contributions to order and peace in recognition of and in subjection to the master principle of love. Another lesson we will learn is to grasp and apply definitions fully and completely. At present, often words that leave the furnace of our mind are not always fully baked and misunderstandings arise that make meanings of words relevant only to the user and no one else. Words have such great celestial exertional force that they require one universally accepted contextual frame of reference in order to facilitate its correct environmental application. We will address some of these definition shortcomings.

# Tolerances and Intolerances

This word like so many words encompass an array of principles that all work together like pieces of a well engineered linguistic machinery so as to produce said appropriate systemic effects in inspired thought and purposeful behavioral direction.

At a universal scale, celestial bodies in their gravitational movements will allow a certain amount of variation or tolerance of a specified quantity relative to their speed of orbit, rotational axis, exertion of mass, etc. These tolerances are tightly regulated and counterbalanced by intolerances so as to conform to inflexible, pre existing systemic principles. Planet earths tilted rotational axis allows for yearly seasonal tolerances and intolerances that are predictable and upon which complex biological cycles rely for life. The human heart operates within tightly controlled hormonal, electrophysiological and biomechanical tolerances and intolerances that make its orchestration a thing of beauty. It is because of the way these tolerances definitively operate that imparts confident peace of mind due this life sustaining characteristic. Once the heart, as excellently as it is designed, spend too much time under conditions of intolerances incompatible with life it will soon cease to support life.

Tolerances and intolerances like so many universalized, perfect, finite algorithms share inversely proportional relationships. Meaning, each definition shares in an equal and opposite counterbalancing set of conditional boundaries. One definition cannot correctly exist without related consideration and respectful validation of the other. Tolerances cannot switch places with intolerance since both are purpose driven. Nor can preset systemic boundaries of tolerances and intolerances be conveniently moved, removed, shrunk or expanded without life ending consequences for those ignorant and guilty alike.

To set tolerances involves principles of goodness, specified quantities and uniform dimensions of acceptable and systemic behavior that is open to small variances until it reaches the fences of tolerant forbearance and limits of forgivable understanding. Conversely, intolerances are enacted hypersensitivities and a policing force of absolutely bigoted systemic responses to that which violates the principles of life promoting tolerances. Intolerances are clear on identifiable indiscretions, inconsistencies and incongruent bad behaviors of unprincipled elements. Intolerances by definition must refuse to tolerate that which is individually and collectively threatening to the master principles of self sustaining systemic love, systemic integrity and systemic peace. Unapologetic intolerances are the unflinching determinates and steadfast reminders of why principles are called principles and standards are called standards. The genius of intolerances is in its narrow minded, laser focus on executing its raw dynamic capabilities in the just and chivalrous cause of glorious life maintenance. Intolerance equates to predictable penalties and consequences for checking societal dis eases, coma like spiritual cognition, fatally impacting erratic spiralings of accelerating moral stupidity, ignorance induced death. Intolerances always succeeds because others fail to do what they know to be universally right and true. Principle is success by reason, by purpose, by directive, by honor, by consciousness, by decency, by application, by character, by substance, by design, by all being responsible for all and to all. The opposite of principle is ambiguity, termination, consequence, last act, final curtain. Once anything or anyone moves outside of parameters of tolerances a gestational period of seconds or centuries is initiated before life ending repercussions ensue in tsunami like fashion and is unalterable. How many earthly celestial bodies think they are being good and tolerant yet are emitting identifiable frequencies of intolerance to goodness that by definition bear a low resonance out of phase with higher dynamic frequency of principle? For every moment that humanity spends in real estate of intolerance the gestational clock is ticking.... world chaos, turmoil, struggle, disharmony, morbidity, mortality. All due to undiagnosed psychosis of toying with and being fixated upon "rights" to move boundaries of tolerances and intolerances put in place to sustain life and make stable, safe conditions for all possible.

## Education and Ignorance

Like black and white, darkness and light, substance and absence these contrasting elements also share a consistent and eternal inversely proportional relationship. Both education and ignorance can be defined by their universal effects. Education is voluntary, considerate, exercises conscience in choices, formulaic in expressing free will, takes responsibility for everything, illuminates and elevates the truthfulness of all matter, its presence is immediately palpable and enriches all it touches. Ignorance is a unsustainable state of being, dense interactional darkness, absence of differential awareness between independence and interdependence, deficiency of character, desperate disposition, lacking knowledge of self, void of understanding relationships and environment, non flourishing mental attitudes, limited perspectives, unconsciously poverty stricken.

All celestial bodies throughout the cosmos behave in a well educated, dignified manner. Each upholds the full scope of defined guiding principles as to what dictates:

- Precise, orderly celestial behavior
- Elegant refinement in dignified satellite function and form
- Unified consensus of strong posture
- Respectful devotion to harmonious purpose
- Responsible and just procession according to requisite law and sound judgement.
- Even noted chaos operates within tightly defined, purposeful, astrophysical etiquette

Our celestial bodies also march in high educated and respectful lock step with each cell of the body also enjoying:

- A unified, committed genetic consensus
- Flourishing intracellular and extracellular harmony
- Expanding awareness of independency and interdependency among systems

- Glorious and responsible recognition of harmonious systemic inequalities relative to successful thriving of organism

When will we take our place of dignity and worth among the stars?

Why are we as galactic citizens of earthly economy not paying attention to their societal responsibility to contribute to their (GPR) Grand Personal Responsibilities and protect THIS right to do what is virtuously and expansively right and fair? Why do inanimate satellites throughout universe act more responsibly and with greater sensitivity to principle and law than humans of greater celestial gifting? When will we awaken from ignorance and educationally elevate our intellectual, moral, ethical, emotional and spiritual capacities? Or are we doomed to remain shackled and plagued in the darkened chambers of our own ignorance, never to see the light of our fullest potentials? Ignorance is not education and education by definition will not cross the boundaries of darkness by virtue of noble blood. To "educe" means to bring out or develop something latent. This implies a strong acting stimulus, an extraction by use of force or pressure relative to an overriding desire to transcend not knowing, not being, not relating to something greater. This is an active, simultaneous, algebraic summation of all our inherent potentials now coming to fruition. Humbling transformational growth, metamorphosis, in sustained fashion takes flight, breaking the chains of limiting ignorance and elevates our spatial deportment as long as we so desire. Our greatest educators of times past have noted that education is not merely about just knowing right things but loving right things as a matter of principle. Education makes the educated a principal in being fully capable of responsible and proper affectation upon adjacent matter. Each one among the educated has now achieved a resonance with the clear role they play in universal peacekeeping. The conscience now fully operational legislates the mental formations of an inner self directing constitution that judges based upon guiding principles. As such, it executes decisions that harmonizes with ultimate good of all bodies relating together in universal gravitation. A congruent inner universe is now reflecting upon and synchronizing with the outer universe.

# Educational hiccups

- If education is not applied evenly to the whole being like a professional paint job, then its work is not complete and our worst human deficiencies are plain to see.

- Just because we are in an information age has no bearing on enlightenment or constitutional transformation of the internal spiritual real estate. All that this means is that we are drowning in knowledge for lack of proper skills and training to swim thru knowledge and attach relevancy and deep meaning to what we do actually grasp and make a part of us. Knowledge, facts and statistics all means nothing if one still orbits around their daily experience crashing into others because they are racist, sexist, and in so many other ways indivisibly ignorant despite daily trajectory thru oceans of data. What is the point of applying educational make up if you are still a pitiful, ugly monster of a human being?

- Being educated in and entertained by rape, torture, murder, violence, etc is only expanding the defined real estate of ignorance. This is a horrible theater in which the worst elements of our inhumanity is now graduating summa cum laude in criminality. We can eminently posit that this is not in any way a good principled education.

- Educational programs often are fundamentally inadequate in that it they only pour knowledge into the mind but do not ascend the steps to full mastery. That being, the mastery of self, the mastery of life skill sets, and most importantly, the practical application of said trainings to the expansion of our personal universe and full enrichment of our personal economies that adds wealth to the world.

Let us leave the real estate of ignorance entirely and not become educated dummies. Educated dummies pat themselves on the back because they can lift mountains of knowledge off library shelves and yet are incapable of identifying self knowledge thru self evaluation and real change. This creature desires more insight into the vast physical universe only to be mentally challenged as to peering insightfully into the composite particles of their own vast inner universe. May we not fancy ourselves civil because we can divine the root of complex mathematical theorems yet remain ignorant of a grander divinity that is even now calculating the square root of our substance, determining merit or malfeasance.

# Love and Hatred

The clearly defined boundaries that characterizes love tolerances as a universalizing principle also shares an inversely proportional relationship with hatred as its counterbalancing non-love equivalence. Hatred owns no love real estate within its preset intolerances. To not grasp loves multidimensional nature is the Shakespearean tragedy of our modern times. The best of who we are and can yet become sacrificed on the flames of wreck less lust parading as love. Although I love the story, I hate its unsavory recurrence in the human drama.

The universe is never in crisis with itself as it applies equally and cumulatively all of the fixed standards that allow for dependable security, desired peace, elegant orderliness from which can be extracted moral consciousness of a permanent, balanced, considerate, loyal love. The human psyche once it is no longer capable of receiving or giving expression of this kind of love dies in spirit long before the body is laid to permanent rest.

Endless space also has built in hatred or intolerances to spatial inadequacies, enigmatic quirks and chaotic manifestations that work against the full scope of loves unifying regulations. The penalties of dissonance are often swift and complete in problematic resolution. The human body is also wired with similar systemically engineered intolerances to alterations in fixed functions, often, with immediate violent countermeasures triggered in response to violated life preserving biologic sanctions.

Human society is experiencing a definitive number of love and hate hiccups and limitations in this area:

- We love, reward and even glorify what we should venomously hate and stand as one against in its eradication.

- We hate what we should emphatically love, perverting innocence and choking justice, asphyxiating unity.

- We vigorously work to blur the two diametrically opposite boundaries of what is love and what is hate and act shocked at the unavoidable and immediate consequences of universal corrective actions taken.

- We too often love only with our sensual, emotional and sexual senses instead of with the entirety of our reasoning being and most expansive definition of stabilizing love.

- We prioritize on romantic fantasies of directing our love attentions on what cannot love us back: technology, mannequins, teddy bears, etc.

- We intellectualize the global sheer necessity to love God and neighbor yet hate the massive inertial forces of work required individually and collectively to implement love meritoriously.

- Whole nations propagandize love while stockpiling ghastly weapons of hate back home. Thereby they advance the idea of using hate to define the very basis for peace while demonizing those who would reason on matters differently.

- We love to flex our free will muscularity but hate the cumulative cramping and pains of kinetic accountability that is anything but free.

Love stops at the boundaries of doing no harm, not violating consciences, not intruding on other people privates, not perversely harming self. Love propagates good, educes the beauty of self actualization and corals such recognized beauty in others. It is a flowering plant, a fruit bearing tree promoting equitable and humane exchange that is mutually respectful. Hatred should rightly proliferate toward anything outside these fluid system dynamics of love.

Love is humanities kindergarten teacher with clear expectations, reasonable demands and sets behavioral grounds for disciplinary actions for those who choose not to play by the rules. If we buckle down and work hard, we could potentially master the basic concepts of the letter and principle of law as well as get excited about building skills of accountability and community responsibility. Love that is misguided leaves its balanced peaceful gravitational orbit and becomes an uncontrolled projectile object whose meteoric mass will ultimately either negatively impact other celestial bodies or burn up from acceleration to unsustainable speeds Love! Love! Love! Love! Love! LOVE! LOVE! LOVE! CRASH!

# Conservative and Liberal

Every element of the universe has qualities, elements and characteristics that can be ultraconservative liberality and ultraliberal conservatism simultaneously. Again, one cannot talk about one without addressing the other counterbalanced ideal. To label anything: any topic, any star or celestial being as one or the other, at best, conveys only a poor fractional synopsis of the circumstances at hand. The two constant forces work in balance as a systemic algorithm of positive and negative decision making feedback loops dynamically driven by changing conditions. These decision making trees intersect and intertwine performing timeless functions, in one moment, free expansion and, in another, defensive reservation. Full adaptation to continual change is fluid with balancing degrees of conservation and progression on an unfathomable scale. The universe is ultraliberal in its expansion while holding to ultraconservative standards, advancing both growth and stability, natural progression and steadfast unity. Destruction of star nebulas can be conservative and preservation liberally principled and right. A mature apple tree has both a root system that firmly plants the tree in the ground and in a good season produces bumper crop yields. The human brain can entertain the same balance of decisional forces in the same meal, ultraconservative stance on vegetables and a strong ultraliberal posture on chocolate cake. Only human society warps these universalizing words and concepts and uses them to wage ideological warfare in concrete and incomplete terms. I despise these degrees in advanced ignorance and have no tolerances for such child's play as an obviously divisive and blinding force out of phase with cosmos.

Copyright protection and Copyright infringement

Powerful universal sanctions protect each heavenly body from having its innate functions altered or infringed upon in any significant way. Copyright protection, in this context, is a cooperative participation in certifying the autonomy of each celestial body in granting it freedom of statutory movement the moment a planet, or nebula is formed. These perceptible and tangible birth rights establish independence and interdependency simultaneously, and is a matter of universal record. The expression of inherent freedom judiciously counterbalanced against and distinguished from not relationally violating the fair and certifiable rights granted others. Each cell of the human body is its own scholar in legislating a intracellular constant of biological law. Each unit of human society has the pure breed right to become scholars of cosmological jurisprudence, training the inner judge and jury to execute ignorance and cross examine structural elements of personal copyright violations. Increasing segments of human society will protest that we are the collective original works of one authorship. As such, the author has strong say so in the methods of our daily operation and can absolutely assert his rights by bringing suit against us for a laundry list of statutory damages highlighting glaring copyright infringements of His intellectual property.

As theoretical physicists and mathematicians continue to amass reams of statistical data many patterns emerge revealing:

No intergalactic waste dumping

No space time unrest

No special particles victims unit

No radioactive wars on terror

No pornographic quasars

No interplanetary mistreatment

No galactic bureaucracy

No bloody religious stellar warfare

No marches over celestial rights

No thermonuclear deliberations over misuse of power

No hitting below the asteroid belt

No inappropriate electromagnetic behavior

No photonic prisons

In conclusion, each one of us is absolutely responsible for the finished product of cosmic citizenship. Lest our lease agreement gets terminated for gross renter misbehavior and extensive destruction of Landlord property, everyone must step up.

The following list will start but by no means complete the universal about face of each individual on this planet:

- Everyone a blacksmith, forging an everlasting edifice of iron determination within each man and woman to stand for goodness.

- Everyone a business person tasked with philanthropically improving the personal economy of our neighbor. Never opportunistically taking advantage of those less fortunate than yourself.

- Everyone an animal trainer taming and bringing into submission all unbridled lusts and misdirected desires so as not to be classed with instinctive beasts.

- Everyone a lawyer upholding legal principle thereby seeking true justice in transcending the letter of the law as to what is morally and ethically righteous.

- Everyone a mountain climber exerting the necessary energy to seek the pinnacle of all our innate human potentials.

- Everyone a police officer so deputized to pull trigger of personal authority on eradicating criminality behind closed doors before it reaches the streets.

- Everyone a clown adding lightheartedness , genuine joy and positivity to serious issues that face us all.

- Everyone a scientist examining the quantitative and qualitative universal evidence of our divine constitution and developing a vision for achieving our, as yet, unrealized abilities garnering the full support of THE Chief Science Officer.

- Everyone a mathematician utilizing with harmonic frequency one grand formulaic moral stand that can be both multiplicatively and indivisibly applied to world conditions at hand.

- Everyone a software architect developing new antiviral software for social changes that bit mines the best of our human constitution and is unhackable.

- Please continue applying all of this to your own experience and thank you responsive cosmic citizen.

# About the Author:

About the author: Robert was born in Brooklyn, New York but raised in St. Petersburg, Florida. Hobbies are reading, working out, and writing when not traveling or engaged in volunteer ministry with his wife Victoria. Twenty two years of nursing has given him unique insights into the human condition that spills out onto the printed page. His favorite Japanese word is kaizen which is translated as "continuous improvement". Really, if one is not improving, growing, and learning everyday then how will one achieve what they were designed to do? Succeed!

Other book titles also by author for purchase thru
Ingram Sparks, Amazon and other fine retailers:

Dances in the theater of the mind

Nurses bred for Business:
The Awakening of Legions of Nurse Entrepreneurs

Foodie Dessertations:
Bite sized recipes of foodielicious poetry

*Coming Soon:*

Positive affirmation lessons for young men

Crouching nurses hidden bedpan:
One nurse that flew over the coo coo's nest poetic
therapy

Success muscle:
Progressive training principles that build success at life

Moneytime Theory:
The missing element in expansion of means

Body systems as business systems:
Build up and maintain both

# Poetry sources I would like to acknowledge:

Oprah's Book Club
Poetry (Magazine)
Poetryfoundation.org
Poetrysoup.com
Academy of American Poets
The Poetry Society of America
Poets & Writers, Inc
Duotrope
New Pages
The Marin Poetry Center
Poets House
The Science Fiction Poetry Association
PennSound
Dallas Poets Community
The Concord Poetry Center
Haiku Society of America
The Poetry Center of Chicago
Star*Line
National Federation of State Poetry Societies
Poetry Journals
Poetry Flash
Arsenic Lobster Poetry Journal
Smartish Pace

Ploughshares
Poet Lore
Poetry Superhighway
Nostrovia Poetry
Cordite Poetry Review
Tule Review
Up the Staircase Quarterly
Slipstream Magazine
Aberration Labyrinth
Plume
Parody
Now Culture
Aberration Labyrinth
The Hollins Critic
Iodine Poetry Journal
Lexicon Polaroid
Abramelin
The Rotary Dial
Chaparral
Blast Furnace
The Araya Review
U.S.1 Poets' Cooperative
Visions-International
Boxcar Poetry Review
My Favorite Bullet

The Innisfree Poetry Journal

Leveler

The Cape Rock

Rattle

32 Poems

491 Magazine

Antiphon Poetry Magazine

Free Verse: A Journal of Contemporary Poetry &
Poetics

Exercise Bowler

Acorn: a Journal of Contemporary Haiku

The Michigan Poet

Toad the Journal

Found Poetry Review

Watermark: A Poet's Notebook

The Poetry Archive

Fishouse

Poetry Quarterly

Poetry Northwest

American Poetry Review

Library of Congress Poet Laureate

All Poetry Blogs

Verse Daily

The Page

The Columbia Granger's World of Poetry

Electronic Poetry Center

Poetry Daily

Button Poetry

Apples and Snakes

Kalamazoo Poetry Festival

Urbana Poetry Slam

Nuyorican Poets Café

Write Out Loud

Geraldine R. Dodge Poetry Program

Chicago Slam Works

The Performance Poetry Preservation Project

Winning Writers

Book That Poet

For Better for Verse

The Writer's Almanac with Garrison Keillor

American Life In Poetry

Wave Books Erasures Tool

Contemporary American Voices